AF259074

I DID SOMETHING WRONG. THEY ALWAYS IGNORE ME.
TAYLOR SEES HER FRIENDS PLAYING VIDEO GAMES ONLINE WITHOUT HER.
THAT'S MY ALARM GOING OFF.
TAYLOR PAUSES, NOTICES THE ALARM, AND BREATHES.
I FEEL LEFT OUT.
SHE ALLOWS AND NAMES HER FEELINGS.
I CAN HANDLE THIS. MAYBE I'LL PLAY WITH KENZIE INSTEAD.
SHE USES A COPING SKILL.
WHAT PROOF DO I HAVE?
WHAT ELSE COULD BE TRUE?
SHE ASKS HERSELF QUESTIONS TO SEARCH FOR THE FACTS.
AND SHE ENCOURAGES HERSELF WITH HELPFUL THOUGHTS.

Think about what you've learned about each letter of the P.A.U.S.E. strategy. Write or draw what each step means.

WHAT I KNOW NOW

Take a moment to notice and celebrate how much you've learned!
Finish these sentences in any way that feels right to you:

One thing I understand about myself now is:

____

____

When my alarm goes off, I want to remember:

____

____

A tool I learned that helps me the most right now is:

____

____

Something my Encourager would want me to know is that:

____

____

MY GAME PLAN

A situation that usually triggers my alarm is: _______________________

____

____

First, I will **pause, notice my alarm, and take a deep breath**. Signs

my alarm is going off are: ______________________________________

____

An unhelpful thought my alarm likes to shout is: ___________________

____

I will **allow and name my feelings** and then **use a coping skill** like:

____

Then I will **search for the facts** by asking myself questions like:

____

____

Last, I will **encourage myself with helpful thoughts** like:

____

____

Remember, you can come back to this plan anytime. The more

you use it, the easier it gets!

PROGRESS, NOT PERFECTION

Experiencing RSD isn't your fault, and it doesn't mean anything's wrong with you. It usually shows up in people who care deeply about relationships and belonging. Your alarm developed to protect you! Sometimes it just gets confused and sounds too quickly and too loudly, but your alarm isn't the enemy, it just needs some guidance. Your alarm will still show up, but now you know what it is, so you can notice it more quickly and recover faster by using the P.A.U.S.E. strategy.

It's helpful to practice your skills during calm moments too. In fact, the more often you practice the skills in this book, the more familiar they'll feel. So, think of a routine you're already doing every single day like waiting for the bus or brushing your teeth. Then try practicing your breathing techniques and coping skills at the same time every day, after you do that same routine.

With practice, your alarm will be able to quiet down sooner, and your Encourager can speak up earlier, helping you respond in ways that make you feel more in control. Practice also helps your muscle memory kick in. Your body will understand, "I know this. I've been here before." So, when feelings show up fast and strong, your tools will be easier to access because you've already been practicing them and they're already a part of your daily routine.

UH OH... THERE'S MY RSD ALARM AGAIN.
FACTS
PAUSE.
BREATHE.
I'VE DEALT WITH MY RSD BEFORE. I CAN HANDLE THIS.
MY ALARM STILL SHOWS UP SOMETIMES. BUT NOW I KEEP GOING BECAUSE I KNOW WHAT IT IS AND WHAT TO DO.

A NOTE FOR FAMILIES & PROFESSIONALS

If you're reading this, you're likely parenting or working with a tween or teen who feels things deeply, reacts strongly to situations that seem small on the surface, or falls apart after moments of feedback, exclusion, or perceived criticism. You may observe intense emotional reactions, sudden shutdowns, anger, tears, or a child who looks confident and capable to others but unravels at home. Many parents describe feeling like they're walking on eggshells or constantly wondering whether they're saying the "right" thing. If this sounds familiar, your child may be experiencing Rejection Sensitive Dysphoria, or RSD.

At the time of this writing, RSD is not a formal diagnosis. It's a neurobiological response to perceived or real rejection, criticism, or loss of connection that many people experience. RSD is more common among neurodivergent folks, especially those with ADHD. It's not a character flaw, a lack of resilience, or a weakness; it's a nervous system that's on high alert for social safety and is working hard to protect connection.

For many tweens and teens with RSD, the brain is wired to monitor social cues very closely. Neutral facial expressions, offhand comments, delayed responses, or small changes in tone can easily be interpreted as signs of disapproval, rejection, or abandonment. When their alarm goes off, the emotional response can be immediate and overwhelming. As William Dodson, MD, explains, "it literally knocks them down." He describes RSD's intensity as being "awful, terrible, and catastrophic... Dysphoria means difficult or impossible to bear. This is not some minor twinge. It's unbearable, emotional pain" (2024).

Brain-imaging studies support this experience. Functional MRI research has shown that social rejection and exclusion activate the same areas of the brain that are involved in physical pain (Eisenberger, Lieberman, & Williams, 2003; Kross et al., 2011). This helps explain why these moments feel so intense and hurt so deeply. When your child reacts strongly, they aren't being dramatic; their brain is responding to a perceived social threat in much the same way it would respond to physical pain.

Over time, RSD can shape behavior in ways that are often misunderstood. Some people cope by overachieving, over-apologizing, people pleasing, or striving for perfection. Some use humor to divert attention and protect themselves. Others withdraw, emotionally shut down, or stop trying altogether. Some internalize the pain through shame and harsh self-criticism while appearing "fine" on the outside. These children may appear to be functioning well on the outside while feeling defeated inside. Others externalize their pain through anger, defensiveness, or explosive reactions. These patterns are all protective strategies developed by the nervous system to avoid the intense pain of rejection and to preserve connection. When we understand these behaviors through the lens of a neurobiological stress response, it becomes easier to shift from "What's wrong with my child?" to compassion, so we can respond more optimally.

Because the alarm response happens so quickly, it often shuts down access to the thinking part of the brain. Logic, reassurance, and problem-solving tend to fall flat in these moments, not because your child is refusing to listen, but because their nervous system is overwhelmed. This is why responses like "just ignore it," "don't take it personally," or "calm down" can unintentionally increase distress. Validating their feelings is critical in these moments, and this doesn't mean agreeing with your child's interpretation of the situation. Validation means acknowledging that their feelings make sense given what they're experiencing.

When someone is sensitive to rejection, their brain may begin constantly scanning for it. A friend sitting with someone else or a neutral look from a teacher can quickly trigger their alarm. Understanding RSD also helps us respond more effectively. When your child's rejection alarm goes off, the most helpful response is safety, not correction. A calm tone, gentle facial expression, slow movements, and sometimes supportive touch can all help with co-regulation. These cues activate the ventral vagal pathway, which elicits feelings of safety and regulates the heart rate, blood pressure, and breathing.

Your family may find it helpful to create a shared language for these moments. A nonverbal signal, visual, or word can communicate when your child's alarm is going off. This reduces shame and power struggles while reminding everyone involved that the reaction is coming from a nervous system in distress, rather than defiance.

The tools in this workbook are most effective when practiced during calm moments, to build muscle memory so they're easier to access when emotions run high. Find time to practice these skills together with your child each day. Make it part of your daily routine by pairing the practice with a habit you already do now, like practicing the skills together every day after you eat dinner.

Many adults also experience RSD, and as you read, you may recognize parts of the RSD experience within yourself. If you experience RSD, supporting a child with RSD can activate your own alarm, especially in moments of criticism, misunderstanding, or helplessness. You can use the P.A.U.S.E. strategy yourself to support your own regulation and model emotional management skills for your family.

Understanding rejection sensitivity doesn't change who your child is, it just changes how supported they feel as they learn to navigate a world that may not always understand them entirely. Your presence, advocacy, and compassion can make an *enormous* difference. You can help your child feel safer, more understood, and more capable of growing through these challenges. Your child will likely need you as an advocate to help educate teachers, coaches, and family members about their RSD experiences. Your support and advocacy can make all the difference!

References

Dodson, W. (2024). ADHD and rejection sensitive dysphoria [Interview]. ADHD Online. https://adhdonline.com/articles/adhd-and-rejection-sensitive-dysphoria/

Eisenberger, N. I., Lieberman, M. D., & Williams, K. D. (2003). Does rejection hurt? An fMRI study of social exclusion. Science, 302(5643), 290–292. https://doi.org/10.1126/science.1089134

Kross, E., Berman, M. G., Mischel, W., Smith, E. E., & Wager, T. D. (2011). Social rejection shares somatosensory representations with physical pain. Proceedings of the National Academy of Sciences, 108(15), 6270–6275. https://doi.org/10.1073/pnas.1102693108

WANT MORE ACTIVITIES AND GAMES TO HELP KIDS COPE WITH RSD?

If you want more supplemental resources and activities to go along with this book, head on over to: www.wholechildcounseling.com/rsd

WHAT DID YOU THINK?

First of all, thank you for purchasing *Skills for Rejection Sensitive Dysphoria*! I know you could have picked any number of books, but you picked this book, and, for that, I am *extremely* grateful. If you found this book helpful, I'd love to hear from you! Please post a review online, tell your friends about it, and share your thoughts on social media. Be sure to tag me so I can repost it too! I'm self-published so your feedback and support is very meaningful to me. It fuels my work and helps spread the word to others.

CONNECTING

To support my work or connect with me, please follow me on social media. You can also go to www.wholechildcounseling.com and join my email list which will give you access to my free social-emotional learning resource library.

ACKNOWLEDGMENTS

This book is dedicated to all the resilient kids I know who experience RSD. I see you and I'm rooting for you every single day. I also want to express my gratitude to my family for their unwavering support, to my editor, Lila LaBine, and to the amazing artist Alejandro Ruisánchez.

ABOUT THE AUTHOR

Casey O'Brien Martin is a passionate person who aspires to bring out the best in each person she works with. She's the author of *Skills for Big Feelings: A Guide for Teaching Kids Relaxation, Regulation, and Coping Techniques*, *Let's Talk About Friendship*, and *Social-Emotional IEP and Treatment Plan Objectives*. She has a Master of Arts in expressive arts therapy and mental health counseling from Lesley University. She is a licensed School Social Worker, a Registered Expressive Arts Therapist, a Licensed Mental Health Counselor, and a Registered Nurse. She has experience working with diverse populations in schools, hospitals, group homes, community centers, and outpatient treatment environments.

Casey considers working with children each day a privilege. Her specialization includes using the arts and a holistic approach to help each child grow as a confident and independent person. She has a longstanding interest in mind/body medicine. She combines her unique background in expressive arts therapy, nursing, and mental health counseling, with herbalism studies to craft comprehensive mind-body programs to help each child reach their highest potential. To learn more about her work, please visit http://www.wholechildcounseling.com.